ANCIENT GREECE

BY GEORGE COTTRELL

UNLOCKING ANCIENT CIVILISATIONS

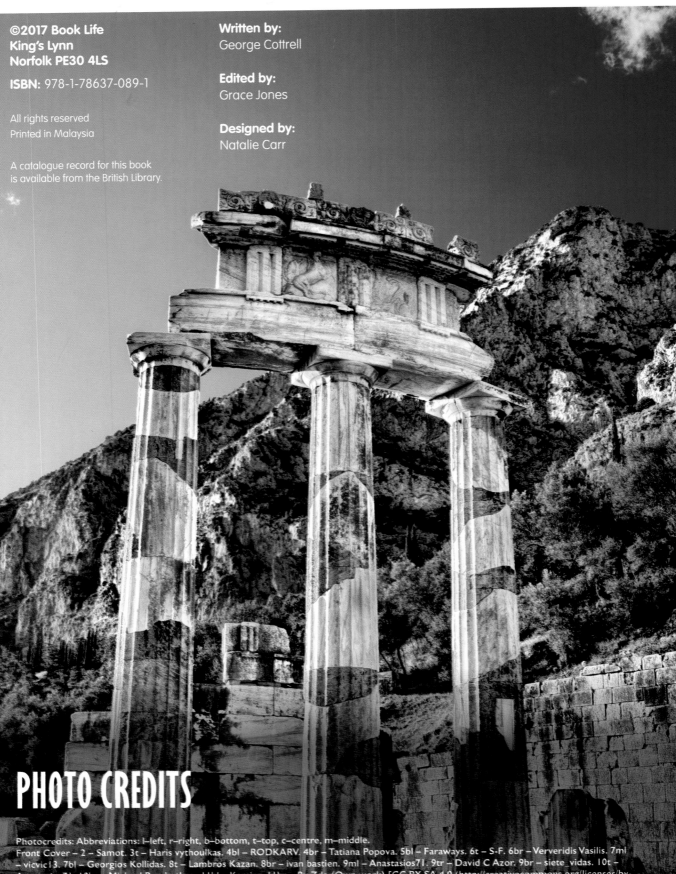

©2017 Book Life
King's Lynn
Norfolk PE30 4LS

ISBN: 978-1-78637-089-1

A catalogue record for this book
is available from the British Library.

Written by:
George Cottrell

Edited by:
Grace Jones

Designed by:
Natalie Carr

PHOTO CREDITS

ANCIENT GREECE

CONTENTS

All words that appear like *this* are explained in the glossary on page 31.

THE ANCIENT GREEKS

THE MYCENAEANS

The first people to rule Ancient Greece were called the Mycenaeans. They ruled over mainland Greece from 1600 – 1200 *BC*. The Mycenaeans were great warriors and brought wealth to the area through *trading*. However, they eventually entered a period of decline in 1200 BC, which we now call the Dark Ages. During this time, people seemed to lose interest in wealth, culture and technology.

THESE ARE THE RUINS OF MYCENAE. MYCENAE WAS AN IMPORTANT SETTLEMENT IN SOUTHERN GREECE DURING THE MYCENAEAN PERIOD.

THE Ancient Greek *civilisation* is thought of by *historians* as one of the most important civilisations in history. The Ancient Greeks developed many new ideas and made great progress in science, culture and the arts. It is because of this that historians often call Ancient Greece the 'cradle of *Western* civilisation'. This means that the Ancient Greeks are seen as the people who began to develop many of the ideas that are the basis of modern life and culture.

It was the Mycenaeans who, according to the Greek poet Homer, were involved in the Trojan War. It was during this war that the famous, wooden Trojan Horse was used to sneak Greek soldiers into the city of Troy.

THIS IS A COPY OF THE ORIGINAL TROJAN HORSE.

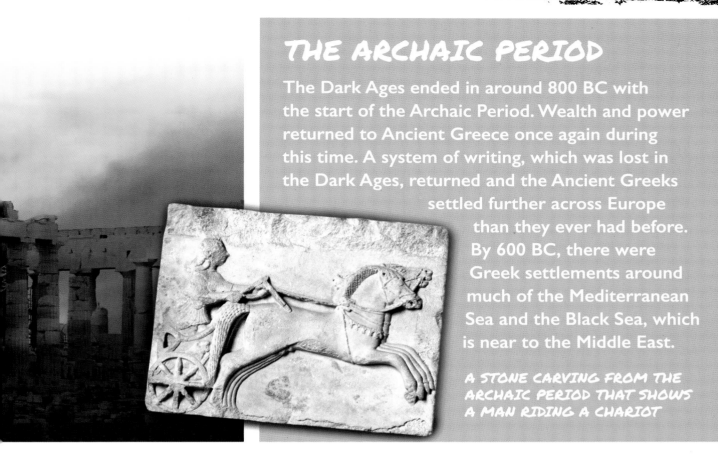

THE ARCHAIC PERIOD

The Dark Ages ended in around 800 BC with the start of the Archaic Period. Wealth and power returned to Ancient Greece once again during this time. A system of writing, which was lost in the Dark Ages, returned and the Ancient Greeks settled further across Europe than they ever had before. By 600 BC, there were Greek settlements around much of the Mediterranean Sea and the Black Sea, which is near to the Middle East.

A STONE CARVING FROM THE ARCHAIC PERIOD THAT SHOWS A MAN RIDING A CHARIOT

Each Greek settlement had its own **government**. The country was divided up into separate city states that were usually ruled by small groups of rich **noblemen**. However, many people were unhappy with the noblemen and this eventually led to a **revolution** and a change in the way that Greece was governed. This change introduced the idea of **democracy** to the world.

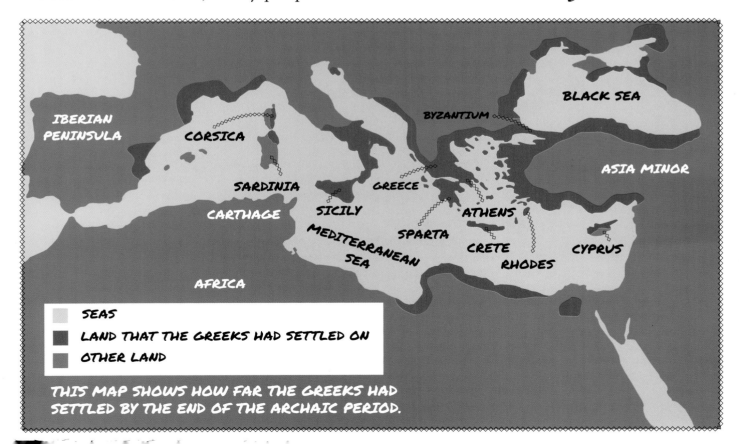

IBERIAN PENINSULA

CORSICA

SARDINIA

CARTHAGE

SICILY

MEDITERRANEAN SEA

GREECE

SPARTA

BYZANTIUM

BLACK SEA

ASIA MINOR

ATHENS

CRETE

RHODES

CYPRUS

AFRICA

- SEAS
- LAND THAT THE GREEKS HAD SETTLED ON
- OTHER LAND

THIS MAP SHOWS HOW FAR THE GREEKS HAD SETTLED BY THE END OF THE ARCHAIC PERIOD.

THE CLASSICAL PERIOD AND DEMOCRACY

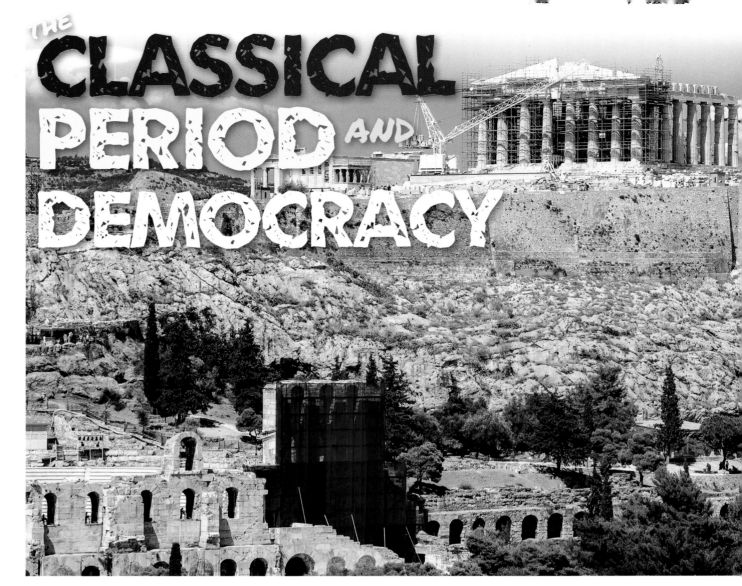

N around 500 BC, the Classical period began and it lasted until 323 BC. This period is known for being the period of time when Ancient Greece was at its strongest, both in culture and military strength. The start of the Classical period in Greece is marked by the introduction of democracy in 508 BC.

DEMOCRACY

Even before democracy, Greek society was made up of citizens and non-citizens. Citizens were men who were born in their city, while non-citizens were women, *foreigners* and slaves. Democracy gave every citizen a say in the government and was first introduced in Athens.

THE ACROPOLIS, AN AREA IN ATHENS WHERE MANY BUILDINGS WERE BUILT DURING THE CLASSICAL PERIOD.

The introduction of democracy also brought about the use of the dikasteria. These were courts that were used to settle *legal* cases in Ancient Greece. The Ancient Greeks used the dikasteria to hold trials using a *jury* made up of about 200 citizens. The jury would have been picked through a process of random selection.

The Classical period in Ancient Greece was also marked by many wars against foreign *invaders* as well as by fighting between the Greek city states. In 490 BC the Persians invaded Greece, starting a period of fighting that lasted until 449 BC. Then, in 431 BC, the Peloponnesian War began. This was a series of battles between the city states of Athens and Sparta.

THIS IS A DRAWING OF THEMIS, THE GREEK GODDESS OF JUSTICE.

THIS IS A DRAWING OF A FAMOUS SPEECH GIVEN BY PERICLES, AN IMPORTANT MEMBER OF ATHENS' GOVERNMENT, AT THE END OF THE PELOPONNESIAN WAR.

ATHENS AND SPARTA

ATHENS

Athens was ruled by its people as a democracy. This meant that the citizens of Athens chose their own ruler. Built under the Acropolis hill and the Parthenon, Athens was known as a centre for education and learning. From 479 BC to 431 BC, Athens enjoyed a period known as the Golden Age when people's interest in science, *philosophy* and the arts grew.

THE two most important and powerful city states in Ancient Greece were Athens and Sparta. The two states were quite close together, only 100 miles apart. However, the way that people in Athens and Sparta lived their lives was very different from one another and this led to a fierce *rivalry* between the two city states.

Sparta was ruled by two kings who came from two different families. It was the only city state to have its own army and life was focussed on this. Male Spartan children began their army training when they were just seven years old and the Spartan army was known to have the best and bravest soldiers in all of Greece.

A SPARTAN SOLDIER'S HELMET

THIS IS A STATUE OF LEONIDAS, ONE OF SPARTA'S MOST FAMOUS KINGS.

For many years, the Spartans helped to protect Ancient Greece. One of their most famous battles was the Battle of Thermopylae in 480 BC, where they fought the Persians. However, Athens wanted more control over the Spartans. This led to a war between Athens and Sparta, which the Spartans eventually won. However, Sparta did not destroy Athens. Because of this, Athens grew to become the most famous of all of the Greek cities.

THE PARTHENON

2,500 years ago, the Persians invaded Athens and left the city in ruins. When the Persians were finally defeated, the Greeks rebuilt Athens. One of the most impressive buildings that was built during this time was the Parthenon. Completed in 432 BC, it was a temple dedicated to the goddess Athena.

THESE ARE THE RUINS OF THE ANCIENT CITY OF SPARTA.

EVERYDAY LIFE

UNLIKE other ancient civilisations, the Ancient Greeks could not survive on their own as they did not have **fertile** land that they could farm. The weather was too hot and dry and there were too many mountains. Instead, they found new homes away from mainland Greece or traded the crops they could grow, such as olives and vines, for grain and other goods that were in short supply. This wasn't a bad thing, as the trading routes they built brought a lot of money into Ancient Greece.

A DRAWING OF AN ANCIENT GREEK SHIP

The Greeks had to sail a lot in order to trade with people across the Aegean sea. This helped them to become great sailors and eventually led to them having a very powerful *navy*. One of the Ancient Greek's greatest military victories was at Salamis in 480 BC when they defeated the Persian navy.

Marriages were usually arranged between families and the women would not have had a say in the decisions. Women would look after the house and family. Wealthier families would often **employ** female slaves to help the women around the house, while male slaves would help to protect the house and teach the family's children.

The Ancient Greeks lived in houses made of stone or clay, with roofs made out of tiles or reeds. The floors were tiled to keep them cool. Men and women would live in different parts of the house, which would usually be built around a courtyard that would act as a centre for family life.

THIS IS AN ANCIENT GREEK COLUMN. THESE COLUMNS WERE THE BASIS OF MANY LARGE GREEK BUILDINGS.

GREEK CULTURE

THE cultural achievements of the Ancient Greeks are some of the most important of any ancient civilisation. During the course of the civilisation, especially during the Classical period, the Ancient Greeks introduced cultural ideas that still exist throughout the world today.

As the Ancient Greeks learnt more about the world around them, they also began to question it. Some people spent their entire lives learning, teaching and asking questions. These people were called philosophers, which in Greek means 'lovers of wisdom'.

Philosophers would gather in small groups in order to try to answer important questions that affected everybody, such as: 'What is a good man?' and 'How can we be happy?'. Even today, the writings of Ancient Greek philosophers such as Plato, Aristotle and Socrates are seen as the starting point of much of Western philosophy and culture.

SOCRATES AND PLATO

Socrates (469 BC – 399 BC) was a great philosopher and teacher. He was admired by his pupils, but the Greek authorities sentenced him to death by drinking poisonous hemlock because his beliefs questioned the gods. Plato was his greatest pupil. When Socrates died, Plato wrote down many of his ideas along with his own. Plato's works are still *influential* today.

A STATUE OF PLATO

ANCIENT GREEK MYTHS

The Ancient Greeks told stories about their gods for entertainment and to help them to understand the world around them. These stories were called myths and they were spread by word of mouth – normally by travellers who would tell stories in every town that they stopped in.

THESE ARE DRAWINGS OF SOME OF THE MYTHICAL CREATURES THAT APPEAR IN ANCIENT GREEK MYTHS.

There were myths told about all sorts of things, such as heroes, wars and imaginary creatures. While the details of the myths would often change depending on who was telling it, the message of the story would always remain the same. Ancient Greek myths are still famous today and they are an important part of Western culture.

THE LABOURS OF HERACLES

Heracles, who was the son of Zeus and was half-man, half-god, had to complete 12 tasks in order to become *immortal*. One of these tasks was to kill the Hydra – a nine-headed serpent. Each time Heracles cut off one of the Hydra's heads, it regrew two more. Eventually, with the help of his friend Iolaus and a flaming torch, Heracles killed the Hydra. However, this was only the second task out of 12!

HERACLES BATTLING THE HYDRA

THESEUS AND THE MINOTAUR

Prince Theseus promised to kill the Minotaur – a half – man, half-bull creature who lived in a maze in Crete – when he was sent as a *sacrifice* to the Minotaur in order to keep Athens safe. Theseus took with him a sword and a piece of string. Eventually, he heard the Minotaur breathing nearby and killed it, dodging the monster's deadly horns. With the Minotaur dead, Theseus followed the piece of string he had laid out behind him and escaped the maze.

AN ILLUSTRATION OF THESEUS KILLING THE MINOTAUR

LANGUAGE AND WRITING

THE RUINS OF THE MINOAN PALACE OF KNOSSOS

THE Minoans of Crete first developed a system of writing in 2000 BC that used **hieroglyphs**. The Mycenaeans followed this with their own written language in around 1400 BC. However, it was not until the Archaic Period, in 800 BC, that the famous Greek alphabet started to be used. Ancient Greeks all spoke the same language, but people in different areas of the country often spoke with different accents.

As the Ancient Greeks spent a lot of time studying science and maths, many letters from the Greek alphabet are used as *symbols* in these subjects today. One example is the use of the letter π (pi), which is now used in lots of mathematical sums. The Latin alphabet, which is used by many modern languages today, such as English, Spanish and French, was heavily influenced by the Greek alphabet.

ANCIENT GREEK WRITING CARVED INTO STONE

The Ancient Greeks used their language and system of writing for many things, including writing Athens' laws onto stone. Because of this, it was important for people to be able to read.

Children were encouraged to learn how to read from a young age. In Athens, boys began school at the age of seven, while in Sparta both boys and girls were educated.

POETRY AND LITERATURE

Another product of Ancient Greek writing was some of the earliest and greatest works of *literature*. In around 800 BC, the poet Homer produced his two poems, The Iliad and The Odyssey. The Iliad was about the Trojan War and the battle between its heroes, Achilles and Hector. Later, during the Classical period, many other famous Ancient Greek authors, such as Sophocles and Plato, also produced writings.

A STATUE OF HOMER

ALEXANDER
THE GREAT

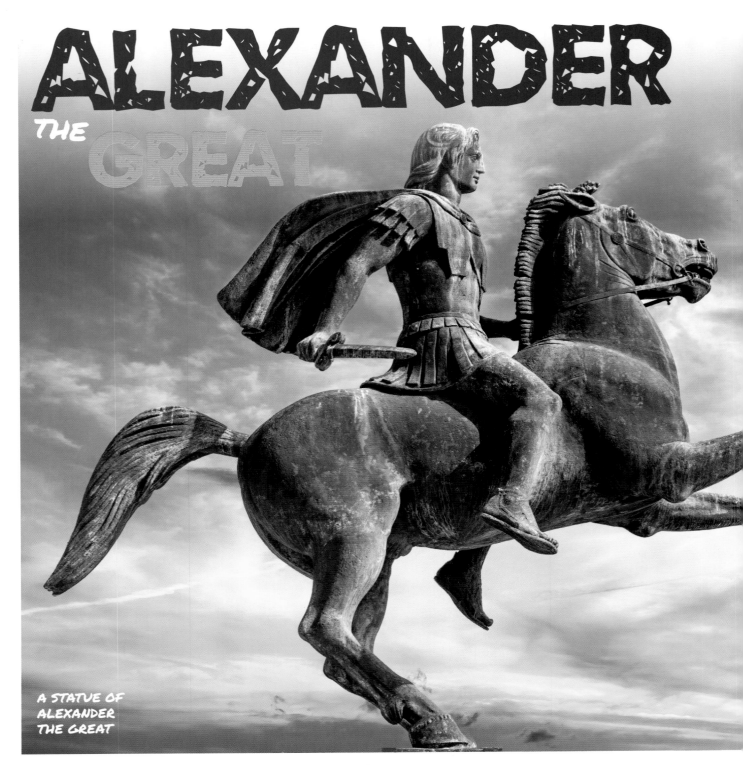

A STATUE OF
ALEXANDER
THE GREAT

ALEXANDER the Great is one of the most famous leaders in Ancient Greek history even though he was actually from Macedonia, a northern part of the Greek Empire. Born in 356 BC, he was the son of King Philip II who had built Ancient Greece into a strong and ***united empire***. Philip made sure that Alexander had the best possible education and that he was taught by the famous philosopher Aristotle.

When King Philip II was *assassinated* in 336 BC, Alexander took to the throne and became one of the greatest leaders the world has ever seen. Reuniting the city states of Ancient Greece, he quickly won the trust of the Greek people and the Greek army.

ALEXANDER THE CONQUEROR

Alexander made the Greek Empire one of the largest empires ever seen, bigger than even the great Roman Empire that was to follow. Many historians think he was the best military leader in history. This is because Alexander managed to conquer the Persians in 333-331 BC and reached as far as north-west India in 326 BC.

It is partly because of Alexander that Greek culture spread so far across the world. Although Alexander was a conqueror, he tried to make sure that the places he ruled over did not hate their new Greek rulers. He did things such as wearing Persian clothing and marrying a Persian princess. In India, Greek influences can be seen in art and sculpture because of Alexander.

A GOLD COIN PICTURING ALEXANDER THE GREAT FROM THE 3RD CENTURY BC

SEAS

LAND ALEXANDER THE GREAT CONQUERED

OTHER LAND

MACEDONIA

BLACK SEA

ASIA MINOR

ATHENS

MEDITERRANEAN SEA

JERUSALEM

BABYLON

PERSIA

PERSEPOLIS

ALEXANDRIA

PALESTINE

RED SEA

GODS, GODDESSES AND RELIGION

A STATUE OF ATHENA, THE GREEK GODDESS OF PHILOSOPHY AND WISDOM

JUST like many other ancient civilisations, the Ancient Greeks believed in lots of different gods and goddesses. They worshipped the gods because they believed that they watched over people and controlled what happened in the world. To show their respect to the gods, they built large and beautiful temples for them.

A STATUE OF APHRODITE, THE GODDESS OF LOVE

The Ancient Greeks also believed that offering sacrifices would help to please the gods. These sacrifices were normally offerings of wine and animals. Priests and priestesses would ensure that the sacrifices were carried out correctly.

Although the Ancient Greeks built temples to worship the gods, they also had many other ways of showing their belief in the gods. The Greeks worshipped at home at small shrines and held festivals to celebrate the gods. The Panathenaea was one of the biggest festivals. It was held every four years in order to honour the goddess Athena.

A STATUE OF ZEUS, THE SUPREME GOD

THIS IS MOUNT OLYMPUS AS IT LOOKS TODAY.

MOUNT OLYMPUS

Mount Olympus is the highest mountain in Greece. The Ancient Greeks believed that the most important gods lived here in luxury, such as Zeus, the supreme God; Hera, his wife; and Aphrodite, the goddess of love. They thought this because Olympus was the place on Earth that was nearest to the heavens.

THE OLYMPIC GAMES

THIS IS A STATUE SHOWING AN ANCIENT OLYMPIC DISCUS THROWER

THE ENTRANCE TO THE ANCIENT OLYMPIA STADIUM

THE Olympic Games began in Ancient Greece. They were held every four years to honour the king of the gods, Zeus, in the Greek city of Olympia. The very first Ancient Olympic Games were held in 776 BC.

Athletes from the different city states of Ancient Greece would compete against each other during the games. The Olympics were so important that there would be a *truce* between the city states to allow people to get to the Games. During this truce, wars would stop and armies would not be allowed to fight.

The Ancient Olympic Games were held in a stadium and had just a few events. These included a chariot race and jumping. Ancient Greek tradition meant that the athletes competed naked.

The Games were not just a sporting event. It was an important religious festival that celebrated the gods and artists and poets helped to record the amazing sporting achievements. It is this idea of the Olympic Games as a large community event, where people from different places come together, that inspired the first modern Olympic Games. First held in AD 1896 in Athens, the modern Olympic Games have become an important part of our modern society, just like in Ancient Greece.

THESE ARE THE OLYMPIC RINGS, WHICH ARE THE LOGO FOR THE MODERN OLYMPICS.

THE END OF ANCIENT GREECE

THE death of Alexander the Great in 323 BC is believed by many historians to mark the beginning of the decline of Ancient Greece. The leaders of Alexander's army killed his *heirs* and split the Greek lands between themselves, after battling for control from 323 BC – 281 BC. These battles marked the end of the Classical period and the beginning of the Hellenistic period.

THIS TEMPLE IN ARMENIA, CALLED THE GARNI TEMPLE, WAS BUILT DURING THE HELLENISTIC PERIOD.

Despite a brief period of success, particularly in Egypt where trading was successful and Greek culture continued to spread, the ***division*** of the empire made the Greeks weak. As a result, the growing Roman Empire took control of Greece and Macedonia in 147 BC.

This was eventually followed by the Roman invasion of the Seleucid Empire in Persia in 64 BC. The final Hellenistic kingdom, Egypt, fell to the Romans in 30 BC, marking the end of Ancient Greece, a civilisation that had lasted for almost 2,000 years.

THESE ARE THE RUINS OF APAMEA, A CITY IN THE SELEUCID EMPIRE.

THE LEGACY OF ANCIENT GREECE

WHILE some ancient civilisations have influenced only small parts of modern society and everyday life, the *legacy* of Ancient Greece can be seen in almost every part of the world around us today. Democracy, science, medicine, *architecture* and philosophy are just a few of the areas in which the Greeks' legacy is still felt.

MATHEMATICS + SCIENCE

Much of what we know about modern mathematics and science was first discovered by the Ancient Greeks. Pythagoras, perhaps the most famous Ancient Greek *mathematician*, discovered a method to find out how long each side of a right-angled triangle was. Called Pythagoras' theorem, it is still taught to children at school today.

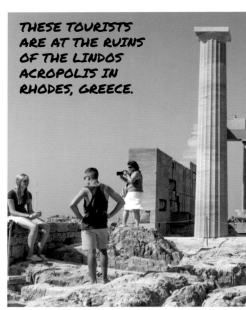

THESE TOURISTS ARE AT THE RUINS OF THE LINDOS ACROPOLIS IN RHODES, GREECE.

ARCHITECTURE

Structures, buildings and temples in Greece were large and impressive. Large columns became an important part of the style of Greek architecture and continued into Roman architecture. In most modern cities today you will find buildings built using these large, impressive columns.

THE BRITISH MUSEUM IN LONDON, ENGLAND IS A PERFECT EXAMPLE OF THE INFLUENCE OF ANCIENT GREEK ARCHITECTURE.

The Ancient Greeks were the first people to perform plays. Thousands of people would watch on steps built into hillsides, called auditoriums. To this day, auditoriums are used by people to watch plays and musical entertainment. Every play written since the time of the Ancient Greeks can be linked to Greek plays – even Shakespeare's!

THE RUINS OF AN ANCIENT GREEK AUDITORIUM

TIMELINE OF A

1600 BC - 1200 BC

>

THE MYCENAEANS RULE ANCIENT GREECE

1250 BC

>

THE TROJAN WAR

1100 BC - 800 BC

>

THE ANCIENT GREEK 'DARK AGES'

500 BC - 323 BC

>

THE CLASSICAL PERIOD OF ANCIENT GREECE

490 BC - 449 BC

>

THE PERSIAN WARS

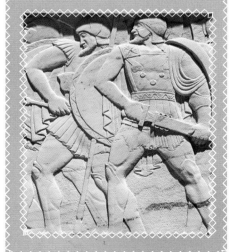

431 BC - 404 BC

>

SPARTA AND ATHENS BATTLE DURING THE PELOPONNESIAN WARS

NCIENT GREECE

800 BC
❯
THE BEGINNING OF THE ARCHAIC PERIOD

776 BC
❯
THE FIRST OLYMPIC GAMES ARE HELD

508 BC
❯
DEMOCRACY BEGINS IN ATHENS

323 BC
❯
ALEXANDER THE GREAT DIES

146 BC
❯
THE ROMANS CONQUER GREECE

30 BC
❯
THE LAST HELLENISTIC KINGDOM, EGYPT, FALLS TO THE ROMANS

MAP OF ANCIENT GREECE

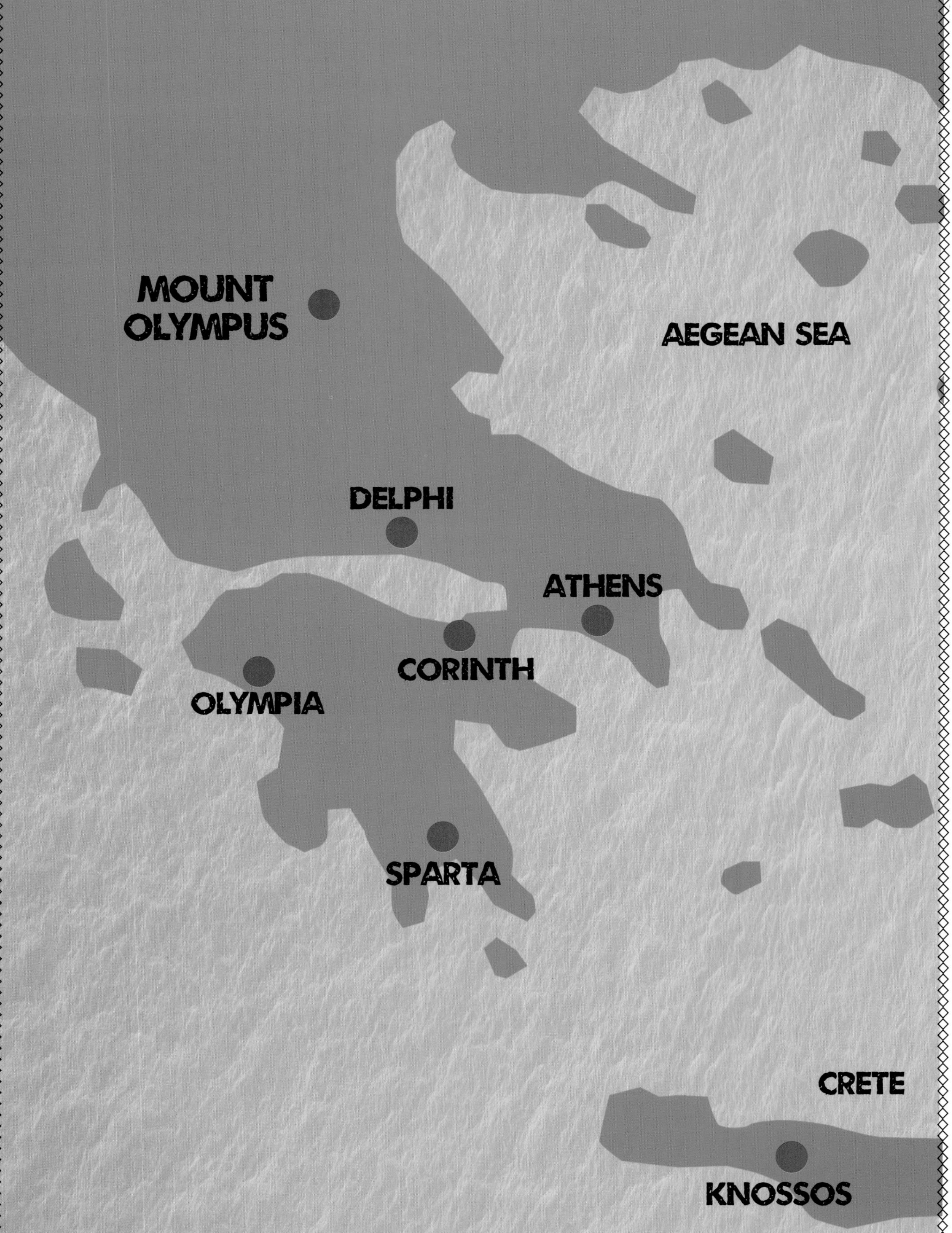

MOUNT
OLYMPUS

AEGEAN SEA

DELPHI

ATHENS

CORINTH

OLYMPIA

SPARTA

CRETE

KNOSSOS

GLOSSARY

architecture	the process and product of planning, designing and constructing buildings or structures
assassinated	to have killed a person, usually by surprise attack
BC	stands for 'before Christ' and means the number of years before the birth of Jesus Christ
civilisation	a society that is very advanced
democracy	a type of government based on the belief that everyone is free and equal
division	a difference or disagreement between two or more groups
employ	to give work to someone
fertile	capable of being used to grow plants and crops
foreigners	people from other countries
government	the group of people with the authority to run a country and decide its laws
heirs	people who legally gain ownership of other people's property when they die
hieroglyphs	the writing system used by the Ancient Egyptians
historians	people who study history
immortal	to be able to live forever
influential	to affect the behaviour of someone or something
invaders	people who attack a country or city in order to try to take it over
jury	a group of ordinary people who go to court in order to fairly decide whether someone has committed a crime
legacy	something handed down from one society to the next
legal	relating to law
literature	written works
mathematician	a person who studies maths
navy	the part of the armed services that deals with ships and the sea
noblemen	people who are part of the highest social class
philosophy	the study of knowledge
revolution	an uprising or rebellion against the government
rivalry	competition
sacrifice	to kill an animal or a human as an offering to a god
symbols	things that represent something else, usually an object that represents an idea or concept
trading	the process of buying and selling goods
truce	agreement of peace
Western	relating to the West, in particular Europe or the United States of America

INDEX

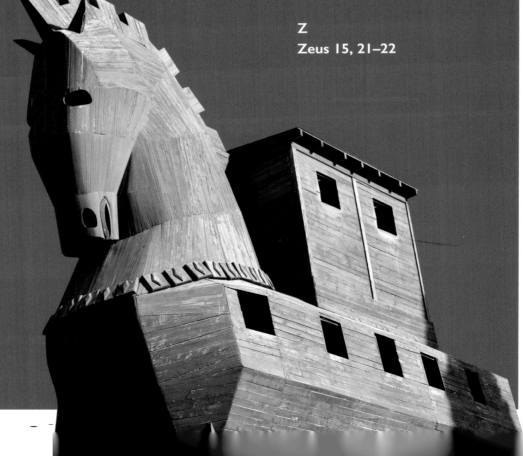